M000011712

NAVPRESS

Discipleship Inside Out™

NavPress is the publishing ministry of The Navigators, an international Christian organization and leader in personal spiritual development. NavPress is committed to helping people grow spiritually and enjoy lives of meaning and hope through personal and group resources that are biblically rooted, culturally relevant, and highly practical.

For a free catalog go to www.NavPress.com
or call 1.800.366.7788 in the United States or 1.800.839.4769 in Canada.

31 Verses EVERY TEENAGER SHOULD KNOW

CHRIST

BY: BRYAN GILL

NAVPRESS

Discipleship Inside Out

table of contents

INTRO

Thank you for choosing this book. I know that you could have chosen any other book in the world to read, but you chose this one. (Okay, maybe not any book in the world, but you get the picture.)

Who would you say is the most important person you know? You probably know about Miley Cyrus, A-Rod, Ashley Tisdale, and Tiger Woods. But the odds are that you really don't know them. You've heard about them and even read about them, but do you know them? You may know all the words to their songs, all their sports stats, and whom they're dating. But do you know them? Maybe you've even met them, but I'll bet that it was only a brief introduction. You probably don't have a relationship with them. You don't really know them.

What if I told you that Jesus is the most important person of all time? That's right. All time. Even before He was born, people were looking for Him. And the world has never been the same since He arrived. Even our historic calendar is centered on Him; B.C. means "before Christ." Now, I understand that you might know about Jesus. But do you really know Him? After reading this book, you will definitely know more about Jesus, but that is not the only purpose of this book. This book is designed to invite you into a relationship with Him.

If you read all of the devotions in here (and I hope that you will), you will see that even before Jesus was born that people were expecting Him. The prophets of the Old Testament wrote about Jesus hundreds of years before His birth. Some 2,000 years later, people are still talking about Jesus.

With all that said, I personally invite you to read these devotions with an open mind. Jesus wants to have a relationship with you. If you read this book knowing that the most important person ever desires to have a relationship with you, your time will be well spent.

Your friend,

Bryan Gill

how to use

Now that you own this incredible little book, you may be wondering, "What do I do with it?"

Glad you asked. The great thing about this book is that you can use it just about any way you want.

It's not a system. It's a resource that can be used in ways that are as unique and varied as you are.

A few suggestions . . .

THE ONE MONTH PLAN

On this plan, you'll read one devotional each day for a month. This is a great way to immerse yourself in the Bible for a month-long period. (OK, we realize that every month doesn't have 31 days. But 28 or 30 is close enough to 31, right?) The idea is to cover a lot of information in a short amount of time.

THE SCRIPTURE MEMORY PLAN

The idea behind this plan is to memorize the verse for each day's devotional; you don't move on to the next devotional until you've memorized the Scripture you're on. If you're like most people, this might take you more than one day per devotional. So this plan takes a slower approach.

THE "I'M NO WILLIAM SHAKESPEARE" PLAN

Don't like to write or journal? This plan is for you. . . . Listen, not everyone expresses themselves the same way. If you don't like to express yourself through writing, that's OK. Simply read the devotional for each verse, then read the questions. Think about them. Pray through them. But don't feel as if you have to journal if you don't want to.

THE STRENGTH IN NUMBERS PLAN

God designed humans for interaction. We're social creatures. How cool would it be if you could go through 31: Christ with your friends? Get a group of friends together. Consider agreeing to read five verses each week, then meeting to talk about them.

Pretty simple, right? Choose a plan. Or make up your own. But get started already. What are you waiting for?

VERSE 1

For God so loved the world that he gave his one and only Son, that whoever believes in him shall not perish but have eternal life. *John 3:16*

In the last few years there have been some high-profile stories of mining accidents in the news. Many of these involved mineshafts collapsing, which trapped miners thousands of feet below the earth's surface. Can you imagine how helpless those miners must have felt? There was nothing they could do to save themselves. They knew that help could only come from someone else.

Have you ever felt completely helpless? I don't mean the way you felt when you didn't study for a test or when you walked out of the restroom with toilet paper stuck to your shoe. I'm talking about claustrophobic-like helplessness. (No, that is not the fear of Santa Claus.) If you have ever felt this way, you know that it's no fun.

Read John 3:9–16. Nicodemus was a really smart guy. He knew the laws and history of Israel. So Jesus reminded him of a story found in Numbers 21 about a group of helpless Israelites wandering in the desert. Soon they got restless and started cursing Moses and God (which is never a good idea). Before they knew it, poisonous snakes had swarmed their camp, and lots of people were dying from being bitten. The Israelites begged for God to save them. In response, God told Moses to raise a bronze snake on a stick so that when people were bitten they could look at it and be healed.

Jesus retold this story to make a point. He wanted to relate to Nicodemus how He Himself had to be raised up—not on a stick, but on a cross in order to save the world. Jesus' purpose was to rescue the world from sin.

Like miners stuck in a mineshaft, we are all trapped and helpless in our sin. We need a savior. We can't make it out without one. Incredibly, God loved us so much that He gave us the Savior in the form of His only Son, Jesus. The Son of God came here for one reason: to save the world because the world could not save itself.

REFLECT

1. HOW DOES YOUR FAMILY USUALLY SPEND CHRISTMAS? DO YOU EAT SPECIFIC THINGS FOR CHRISTMAS DINNER? DO YOU TRAVEL?

2. NOW THINK OF A CHRISTMAS FROM THE PAST FEW YEARS IN WHICH SOMETHING UNEXPECTED HAPPENED. DID IT MAKE CHRISTMAS BETTER FOR YOU AND YOUR FAMILY? HOW SO?

3. THE PEOPLE OF ISRAEL DIDN'T EXPECT JESUS TO COME AS HE DID. MAKE A QUICK LIST OF ALL THE OUTRAGEOUS THINGS GOD DID TO MAKE SURE THAT EVERYONE DIDN'T MISS JESUS' ARRIVAL.

4. YOU PROBABLY EXPECT GOD TO SPEAK TO YOU IN A FEW WAYS THAT YOU'RE USED TO. ASK GOD TO DO SOMETHING UNEXPECTED TODAY THAT SHOWS YOU IN A FRESH WAY HOW MUCH HE LOVES YOU.

VERSE 3

"The days are coming," declares the Lord, "when I will raise up to David a righteous Branch, a King who will reign wisely and do what is just and right in the land.
Jeremiah 23:5

Other than the lack of modern medicine and the frequent use of beheading, it would be cool to travel back in time to see how great kings and queens ruled. But whether you're watching *King Arthur* or *The Lord of the Rings*, at least one truth cuts across all the portrayals of kingship: All the kings died. No matter how powerful a king might be or how far his kingdom expands, he still dies at some point in his rule. Although the people chant, "Long live the King!" the reality is that his term is only temporary.

Read Jeremiah 23:5–6. The prophet Jeremiah told the people of Israel that a king would come from the line of King David. This king would reign with wisdom and do what is right in the land. The people longed for this good king. Earthly kings came and went for Israel, and so far no one had been the great king they were looking for.

Then Jesus was born from the lineage of David. At last their good king had come! But Israel was under Roman rule at this time. That meant one thing: Jesus was not to be an earthly and political king—but rather an eternal and universal king. Jesus' rule was not just over the Israelites—but over all people. Jesus fulfilled Jeremiah's prophecy of a coming king who would be wise and just. He was the king who would rule not for a temporary term like every other king—but for eternity.

To this day, Jesus still rules with wisdom and justice. Although He died, Jesus' resurrection from the grave allowed him to conquer death. Therefore, His kingship will never die. You cannot make Jesus the King of your life—He already is King. Because of that, your goal is just like that of a loyal knight: to honor and worship the King with the ways that you act, think, and speak.

reflect

1. WHAT TALENTS AND ABILITIES DO YOU HAVE THAT WOULD MAKE YOU A GOOD KING?

2. EVERYONE IS TEMPTED TO BE HIS OR HER OWN SOVEREIGN RULER. HOW DO YOU CURRENTLY TRY TO PLAY THAT ROLE IN YOUR LIFE?

3. WRITE DOWN THE CHARACTERISTICS OF JESUS THAT YOU THINK MAKE HIM SUCH A GREAT KING.

4. HAVE YOU SURRENDERED YOUR LIFE TO SERVE KING JESUS? WRITE A SHORT PRAYER TO JESUS, TELLING HIM THAT YOU ARE HIS SERVANT. SURRENDER ANYTHING IN YOUR LIFE THAT HAS COME BETWEEN YOU AND HIM.

verse 4

For to us a child is born, to us a son is given, and the government will be on his shoulders. And he will be called Wonderful Counselor, Mighty God, Everlasting Father, Prince of Peace. *Isaiah 9:6*

The Lion King is one of my favorite movies. I love the opening scene, especially when Rafiki holds Simba high above his head for all of the animals in the kingdom to see. They _____ been awaiting the birth announcement of the king's son, and at last it was here. The whole kingdom rejoiced when the son was presented to them. There is just something about the fever pitch of hope and excitement in that scene that makes you want to hold your cat high in the air for all the neighborhood pets to see.

The birth announcement for Jesus came several hundred years before he was actually born. That alone shows that this was not your typical "It's a Boy!" announcement. Read Isaiah 9:6–7. This passage says that the entire government will rest on the shoulders of this child and that his reign will never end. He is better than any king before or after—even the beloved and revered King David. Who could fulfill this role of being called Wonderful Counselor, Mighty God, Everlasting Father, and Prince of Peace? As the years passed, some of the Israelites lost hope that they would ever get a king like this. But we know from Scripture that the Israelites' prayers were answered in an incredible way. A Messiah did come. Jesus, God's Son, fulfilled every prophecy ever written.

"So," you ask, "what does that mean for me today?" Good question. First of all, you can know that God is faithful to keep His promises. He promised Jesus. He delivered Jesus. God keeps all of His promises. You can count on Him. Second, Jesus is just who Isaiah said that He would be. Jesus is everlasting. He will not leave you. Jesus is mighty. He is powerful enough to handle all of your doubts and fears. Jesus brings peace. He can bring peace to your soul. And a day is coming when He will bring peace to this world. For good.

REFLECT

1. HOW HAS JESUS MADE A DIFFERENCE IN YOUR LIFE?
THINK ABOUT SOME REAL AND PRACTICAL WAYS THAT
YOUR LIFE HAS CHANGED BECAUSE OF HIM.

2. DO YOU TURN TO JESUS FOR HELP AND GUIDANCE?
IF SO, WHAT HAVE BEEN THE RESULTS? IF NOT, WHAT IS
KEEPING YOU FROM DOING SO?

3. DO YOU KNOW PEOPLE WHO NEED THE PEACE AND REST
THAT ONLY JESUS CAN BRING? PRAY FOR THEM NOW
THAT THEY WILL GIVE THEIR NEEDS, FEARS, DESIRES, AND
PLANS OVER TO CHRIST.

VERSE

"I and the Father are one." *John 10:30*

Family reunions are bittersweet to me. On the one hand, I can't stand it when people tell me that they remember when I was in diapers and when I used to make table art with my peanut butter. On the other hand, I love it when people tell me that I look like my dad. As I grew up, I thought it was cool when people would mistake my voice for my dad's on the phone. One day, after my dad ate lunch with me at my high school, some of my friends came up to me and said, "I couldn't tell the difference between you and your dad when he was here." I considered it an honor to be mistaken for my dad.

Read John 10:22–30. The Jews were angry with Jesus in this passage. They claimed that He would not tell them whether He was the Christ. Jesus, however, answered their question when He told them that He was doing miracles in His Father's name. Jesus went on to say that He and His Father are one. The things that His Father did, He did. The things that His Father said, He said. Jesus claimed that if His Father was doing a miracle, it was Jesus doing the miracle. How could this be? It was because Jesus and His Father are one. The Father and Jesus do not merely resemble each other like I resemble my father—Jesus said, "I and the Father are one."

If people want to know God, they have to get to know Jesus. People cannot know God without knowing Jesus. When you read what Jesus said and pay attention to how He treated people, you're actually getting to know God as well. It's amazing that we can know so much about God by looking at Jesus and His life.

9

reflect

1. THINK ABOUT THE PEOPLE WHOM YOU'D LIKE TO BE MISTAKEN FOR. WHAT ABOUT THEM DO YOU WANT TO LOOK LIKE?

2. MAKE A LIST OF THREE PEOPLE WHOM YOUR FRIENDS SAY YOU RESEMBLE IN ATTITUDE OR PERSONALITY. WHY DO YOU "LOOK" LIKE THEM?

3. IF YOUR BEST FRIENDS MADE A LIST OF THE THINGS YOU DO OR SAY THAT RESEMBLE JESUS, WHAT WOULD THEY SAY? WHAT WOULD YOUR MOM SAY? HOW ABOUT THE PERSON YOU HAVE A CRUSH ON?

4. ASK THREE PEOPLE WHO REALLY KNOW YOU TO MAKE A LIST OF HOW YOU RESEMBLE JESUS. PUT THAT LIST IN A PLACE THAT YOU WILL SEE EVERY DAY TO ENCOURAGE YOU TO KEEP LOOKING LIKE JESUS AND THE FATHER.

verse

The Word became flesh and made his dwelling among us. We have seen his glory, the glory of the One and Only, who came from the Father, full of grace and truth. John 1:14

Road trips are cool. The best part? You get to see lots of places in a short amount of time. We often take road trips to places that we want to visit but probably would never live in. These places may be great to visit for whatever reason, but you wouldn't necessarily want to call them home. It's not like you'd be in a hurry to leave your friends, school, and family to move there.

Read John 1:1–14. This passage speaks about the Word being in the beginning with God. But John doesn't stop there. John says that not only was the Word with God, but the Word was God. What (or who) did John mean when he referred to the Word? This is a reference to Jesus. Jesus was with God in the beginning because Jesus is God.

Verse 14 says that the Word became flesh and dwelled among us. You may have heard of the really churchy phrase: Word incarnate. What this means is that the Word, Jesus, became "flesh" the moment He was born here on earth. Jesus was no longer far away. He was here with real skin and bones, breathing oxygen just like you and me.

The most important part of this passage is the fact that Jesus came to live with us. We do not worship some made-up figure that cannot relate to us. Jesus did not just come and visit us on some heavenly road-trip. He came to do life here with us. He was not simply passing through. He lived, ate, slept, laughed, cried, died, and was even raised from the dead here.

There is nothing that you have experienced here on earth that Jesus didn't experience. He can relate to you in so many ways because He's been where you are.

REFLECT

1. SOMETIMES IT'S EASY TO FEEL LIKE JESUS IS FAR AWAY AND DOESN'T UNDERSTAND WHAT YOU'RE GOING THROUGH. WHAT ARE YOU STRUGGLING WITH THAT YOU FEEL JESUS CAN'T RELATE TO?

2. HOW DOES IT MAKE YOU FEEL TO KNOW THAT JESUS LIVED A HUMAN LIFE WITH ALL OF THE SAME NEEDS AND FEELINGS THAT YOU HAVE? HOW DOES THAT HELP YOU KNOW THAT HE CAN RELATE TO YOU?

3. WHAT'S KEEPING YOU FROM TELLING JESUS HOW YOU'RE FEELING AND WHAT YOU'RE THINKING?

4. IN THIS NEXT SECTION, WRITE A SMALL LETTER TO JESUS, TELLING HIM EVERYTHING THAT HAPPENED TO YOU TODAY. TRUST ME—HE'LL UNDERSTAND. HE'S BEEN HERE ALREADY.

VERSE

7

Then those who
were in the boat
worshiped him,
saying, "Truly
you are the Son
of God."
Matthew 14:33

Think back to the Christian camps or retreats that
you've attended. You probably felt really close to God
while you were there. That's an awesome feeling, isn't
it? The problem is that it's easy for your spiritual high
to last a short time and then . . . go back to normal.
Am I right? You might be surprised, but Jesus' disciples struggled with this as well.

Read Matthew 14:22–33. This must have been one of the coolest days
for a disciple of Jesus. First, they witnessed Jesus feeding thousands of
people with only a little food. A few hours later, they saw Jesus walking on water. However, between the first miracle and the second one,
they doubted that Jesus was God's Son. The Bible says that as Jesus
was walking on the water, the disciples thought that He was a ghost.
Only after Peter tried out his sea legs did they recognize Jesus. When
Peter sank and Jesus brought him back to the boat, the other disciples
declared that Jesus must really be the Son of God. What happened between the miraculous feeding of the thousands and Jesus' water-walk
to change their minds? Why did they doubt?

We do the same thing. Why is it so hard for us to keep that spiritual
high between camps or retreats? Maybe it is not just camps. It might
be Sunday to Sunday or Sunday to Wednesday . . . Peter teaches us
how to believe in those times. He trusted that Jesus would let him walk
on water and that Jesus would save him if he sank. Peter obeyed Jesus
when he was told to walk on water. Peter proclaimed Jesus as God's
Son with his actions. The others did it with their lips.

Talk is cheap and easily fades away. How do your actions demonstrate
to the world your faith in Christ?

reflect

1. IN YOUR OWN WORDS, WHY DO YOU THINK THAT IT IS SO
CHALLENGING TO KEEP YOUR FAITH STRONG BETWEEN THE
SPIRITUAL HIGH POINTS OF YOUR LIFE?

2. WRITE DOWN THREE SPECIFIC WAYS IN WHICH YOU CAN
DECLARE TO THE WORLD AROUND YOU THROUGH YOUR ACTIONS
AND WORDS THAT YOU BELIEVE JESUS IS THE SON OF GOD.

3. PRAY THAT YOUR FAITH WOULD BE STRENGTHENED THROUGH
THE POWER OF THE HOLY SPIRIT. ASK THE SPIRIT TO LEAD YOU
INTO A DEEPER RELATIONSHIP WITH GOD TODAY AND TO KEEP
YOU SOLID THROUGH THE LOW POINTS IN YOUR LIFE.

verse 8

"Ha! What do you want with us, Jesus of Nazareth? Have you come to destroy us? I know who you are—the Holy One of God!" *Luke 4:34*

On July 6, 2008, what most experts have called the greatest tennis match in history was played at Wimbledon. If you're not a tennis fan, you need to know that Wimbledon is the sport's largest event. In that contest, the two biggest stars in men's tennis battled out in a slugfest for the ages, the longest finals match in the sport's history, a match that saw rain, wind, and near-nightfall descend upon the English tournament. The underdog, Spain's Rafael Nadal, beat the favorite, Switzerland's Roger Federer. It was arguably one of the greatest sporting events in history.

Rather than trash his opponent when the match was over, Federer was gracious and full of praise in defeat. "[Nadal] is a deserving champion," Federer said. "He just played fantastically." Isn't it interesting that an opponent would acknowledge the greatness of the individual who had defeated him?

Read Luke 4:31–37. In this passage, a demon-possessed man met Jesus. The demon cried out that Jesus was the Holy One of God. Jesus was so powerful that the demon had to acknowledge Jesus as divine and submit to His commands. It's interesting that even after the demons proclaimed Jesus as holy, the people listening were still unsure as to where Jesus had received His authority. What does that say about the people in the synagogue?

Sometimes it is hard for us to fully comprehend who Jesus really is—the holy Son of God. But Jesus' enemies know exactly who He is! Here's the truth: There is no demonic power that Jesus hasn't overcome. And if Jesus' enemies recognize His power, shouldn't we? If those whom Jesus has completely defeated acknowledge His greatness, shouldn't we (the ones He has saved) do the same?

15

REFLECT

1. DESCRIBE A TIME IN THE PAST WHEN YOU FOUND IT
HARD TO TRUST THAT JESUS HAS THE POWER TO DIRECT
YOUR LIFE AND THE WORLD AROUND YOU.

2. HOW DOES JESUS REMIND YOU THAT HE IS POWERFUL,
HOLY, AND DIVINE?

3. WHAT AREAS OF FEAR IN YOUR LIFE DO YOU NEED TO
SUBMIT TO JESUS' POWER?

VERSE

The men were amazed and asked,
"What kind of man is this? Even the
winds and the waves obey him!"
Matthew 8:27

When I was younger, I loved to play outside. I played every day during
the summer. But my mom wouldn't let me go outside when it rained.
Whenever that happened, I would sing a little song to try to make it stop
raining: "Rain, rain go away, come again another day . . ." It seems a little
silly now, but I thought that it would work when I was a kid. The problem
was that it never worked. No matter how hard I tried to stop the rain, I
didn't have the power to do it.

Matthew 8 tells a story of Jesus and His disciples in a boat. Suddenly, a
storm came upon them, and the disciples were terrified. Jesus asked why
they were afraid (even though He knew that they were freaking out because
of the storm). Jesus knew they didn't fully understand that He was the one
who had created the wind and rain. Unlike my powerless singing as a kid,
when Jesus told the wind and rain to stop—they listened. Look at Matthew
8:23–27 to read the story for yourself.

Nothing surprises God. Not storms, not earthquakes . . . nothing. We
are the only ones caught off guard. The winds obey Jesus and submit to
His authority. And just like the winds, we are to submit as well. See, God
wants us to trust in Him and in His Son, Jesus. That is what the disciples
did. In the middle of the storm, they cried out, "Lord, save us." They
believed in God's power to save them.

We have seen in recent years how people come together after hurricanes
and other disasters. Christians, churches, and youth groups come together to love people and turn to God for comfort during their distress.
God wants us to trust Him even in the midst of storms. Why should we
trust God? Because He is always in control. Always.

reflect

1. HAVE THERE BEEN TIMES IN YOUR LIFE WHEN YOU TURNED TO JESUS AND HE PROVIDED YOU A WAY OUT OF A TRYING SITUATION? WRITE DOWN A SHORT SUMMARY OF WHAT HAPPENED.

2. HOW DID JESUS' DEMONSTRATION OF HIS AUTHORITY IN THIS SITUATION HELP YOU TO DRAW CLOSER TO HIM?

3. WRITE A PRAYER TO JESUS THAT THANKS HIM FOR BEING ACTIVE IN YOUR LIFE. PRAISE JESUS FOR HIS POWER AND AUTHORITY AND FOR HIS WILLINGNESS TO USE IT FOR THE GOOD OF HIS CHILDREN.

verse 10

He is before all things, and in him all things
hold together.
Colossians 1:17

I love video games. Halo™, Guitar Hero™, Rock Band™, and any
of the first-person shooters . . . However, my favorite games are the
ones in which I have complete control. NCAA Football™ and Mad-
den Football™ make me giddy. I like these because I am in complete
control. I hold the controller. If I want to make my team wear black
jerseys, blue shoes, and green helmets, I can do that because I am in
control. If I want to transform myself into a player that is 6'5" and
250 lbs that can run faster than Larry Fitzgerald, I can do that too.
Because I am in control. And being in control is awesome.

Read Colossians 1:15–20. Jesus has real control. As the Son of God,
Jesus has power and authority over the created world (and everything
in it, including power over death and sin). But one of the coolest
aspects of Jesus' role as the Son is that He quite literally keeps all of
creation going. How do you know this? It's that little phrase in verse
17: "in him all things hold together."

The word *sustain* means to hold things together and strengthen. The
whole universe is sustained, held together, kept going, and made
stronger by Jesus. That is serious control!

Jesus' power is real. He does not simply hold a controller. He is the
controller. Not only does He have the power to control all things,
but through His power Jesus holds all things together. Jesus' role as
sustainer is an amazing comfort in our lives. You can be confident
that no matter what happens in the world, Jesus is keeping everything
together and moving toward a future that He has set in motion. Nothing is a surprise to Him. Rest easy. Jesus is in control.

REFLECT

1. DO YOU EVER WORRY ABOUT YOUR FUTURE? OR THE FUTURE OF THE WORLD AROUND YOU? (IT'S OK IF YOU DO—IT'S NATURAL.) IF SO, HOW DOES KNOWING THAT JESUS HOLDS EVERYTHING TOGETHER CHANGE THE WAY THAT YOU FEEL?

2. WHAT AREAS OF YOUR LIFE DO YOU NEED TO TRUST TO JESUS' CONTROL?

3. HOW CAN YOU TRUST THE REALLY PERSONAL THINGS IN YOUR LIFE TO JESUS' CONTROL MORE CONSISTENTLY?

20

VERSE

Those of you who have a license to drive can relate to what I'm about to write. (If you don't have your license yet, then I'm sorry to rub it in.) There are several signs that you have to learn for your driving test, right? But there are two big ones you'll want to remember. The first is the "One Way" sign and the other is the "Wrong Way" sign. "One Way" signs are black with white letters and point in one direction. When you see this sign, you want to make sure that you follow the direction of the arrow. However, if you make a wrong turn down a one-way street, you'll see another sign. It's big and red with "Wrong Way" printed on it. These signs serve as warnings because you are in danger of hitting another car. Trust me. I know from experience. You don't want to see the "Wrong Way" sign.

Read what Jesus says in John 14:1–7. In our passage for today, Jesus is telling His disciples about Heaven and that they already know how to get there. But one of them says to Jesus, "We don't know the way." Jesus replies, "I am the way." If we know Jesus, then we know the way to Heaven. Jesus is literally the only way to get there. He is not a way. He is the "One Way." All other ways amount to the "Wrong Way."

If there was an actual road sign to Heaven, it would be a "One Way" sign pointing to Jesus. If you were to turn away from Christ, then you would see "Wrong Way" signs warning you that danger is ahead. There would be "Wrong Way" signs on the road of "doing all the right things" or "going to church all the time." The only way to get to Heaven is the "One Way" found in faith in Jesus Christ. All other roads lead to dangerous lifestyles and eternal separation from God.

Which way are you headed?

reflect

1. WHAT ARE SOME POPULAR BELIEFS IN THE WORLD TODAY ABOUT HOW TO GET TO HEAVEN?

2. WHAT DO YOU THINK IT TAKES TO GET TO HEAVEN?

3. IF YOU ARE UNSURE OF WHETHER YOU ARE ON THE RIGHT ROAD, TAKE SOME TIME TO TALK TO AN ADULT IN YOUR CHURCH. EXPRESS YOUR CONCERNS TO HIM OR HER. IN THE MEANTIME, TAKE A MOMENT TO WRITE A PRAYER TO GOD THAT EXPRESSES YOUR FEARS AND CONCERNS. ASK HIM TO CONFIRM FOR YOU THAT HE TRULY IS THE PATHWAY TO ETERNAL LIFE.

verse 12

Your attitude should be the same as that of Christ Jesus.
Philippians 2:5

Have you ever heard a guy referred to as "a real man"? Does this mean that he used to be made out of wood and then came to life like Pinocchio? All kidding aside, people use that phrase to refer to their ideal picture of a man. It implies a standard for manhood that's usually associated with toughness, strength, etc. You probably have an image of what you see as an ideal person. This was true for people in Jesus' time, too.

The Jews anticipated the Messiah, God's Son, with great expectation. Many of them envisioned the Messiah coming with political power to rule an earthly kingdom. God had different plans, though. He chose to send Jesus to earth in the form of a helpless child who would grow to be a rabbi to a group of fishermen and tax collectors. Jesus, God in the flesh, ruled in Heaven and sat on His throne as King of the universe. But He gave everything up to become a servant. In that moment, He became a real man—the ideal man.

Read Philippians 2:5–7. Paul, the writer of Philippians, teaches us a great lesson in this passage. He says that we should have the same attitude of humility that Jesus had. If there was anyone who deserved to be treated like a king, it was Jesus. He came to earth, however, to serve. Jesus' life teaches us the power of love and humility.

When we succeed and people applaud us, more times than not we start feeling important. This creates a problem. When we think that we are important, we simultaneously think that other people are less important. That is why Paul's message is so vital for us. If the King of the universe put other's needs before His own safety and comfort, what can we ever achieve that would lead us to think that we are more important than others?

Our attitude should be that of humility . . . just like Christ.

23

REFLECT

1. COMPARE YOUR ATTITUDE TO WHAT YOU KNOW (AND TO WHAT PAUL SAYS) ABOUT JESUS' ATTITUDE. DOES YOUR ATTITUDE IMITATE JESUS' ATTITUDE?

2. WHAT CHANGES DO YOU NEED TO MAKE IN YOUR ATTITUDE FOR IT TO BECOME MORE LIKE CHRIST'S?

3. HOW CAN YOU SHOW HUMILITY EVEN IF YOU FEEL IMPORTANT?

VERSE

"For even the Son of Man did not come to be served, but to serve, and to give his life as a ransom for many."
Mark 10:45

During your next trip to the movies, try this experiment: Wait until you see a really big dude get in line. Then go cut right in front of him. When he taps you on the shoulder (which he definitely will) and tells you to get back to your original spot in line, tell him that you are more important than he is and that he needs to let you go in front of him. If you're lucky enough to wake up after he's done responding to you with his big fists, please tell me how this experiment worked out.

People naturally want their needs met before the needs of others. We think that we are more important than our neighbor. That's the reason the big dude in the movie ticket line would be so unhappy with you for breaking. In his mind, his needs come before yours. But God calls us to reverse this trend.

Take a look at Mark 10:35–45. In this passage, two of the disciples asked Jesus for a favor. Basically, they wanted to be highly regarded in Heaven. Jesus, however, had some very sobering words for them. He said that the officials of their day used (and probably often abused) their authority over people. Jesus then told them that He did not come to Earth to be served but to serve. Jesus knew that service is a hard concept for people to understand, so He came as a servant to show us how to serve.

The way that we can become better Christians is to work on the way in which we serve others. Just as the disciples were expected to put others first, so are we. We are not supposed to be Christians that expect a pat on the back all the time. Christians should serve other people. There is a responsibility that comes with the privilege of being a Christian. This responsibility is to serve others.

reflect

1. ON A SCALE OF 1 TO 10 (WITH 10 REPRESENTING THE BEST), HOW WOULD YOU RATE YOURSELF AS A SERVANT?

2. WHAT ARE SOME WAYS IN WHICH YOU CAN SERVE OTHERS?

3. WHAT AREAS OF SERVICE DO YOU NEED TO WORK ON?

verse 14

"Which is easier: to say, 'Your sins are forgiven,' or to say, 'Get up and walk'?" Luke 5:23

Have you ever done something that you thought was private—but it really wasn't? Steve Carell, as Maxwell Smart, encountered this in the movie *Get Smart*. CONTROL told Smart that they were making him a field agent. Not wanting to show the others how excited he was, he chose to celebrate where no one could hear him—in the Cone of Silence. The Cone of Silence is an invisible chamber inside which, when activated, no one can hear your conversation. Thinking that the other people couldn't hear him, Smart started yelling in jubilee about the news. There was only one problem: He hadn't activated the Cone properly, so everyone could hear him yelling.

The Pharisees in our passage obviously thought that they were in the Cone of Silence around Jesus. The Teacher, however, heard their thoughts.

Read Luke 5:17–26. By the time these guys brought their friend to Jesus, He had healed many people. The crowd had witnessed many miracles up to that point, but they didn't expect to hear what they heard next. The Bible says that when Jesus saw their faith, He told the man that his sins were forgiven. Jesus knew that the Pharisees doubted His ability to forgive sins. They hated Jesus and were always causing trouble. Do you think that they were shocked when Jesus turned to them and told them what they were thinking? Jesus not only heard their thoughts, but He knew their hearts as well.

Sometimes we think that Jesus doesn't know what we are thinking because we do things in private. Jesus, however, knows our thoughts and the condition of our heart. Even if we hide things from people, we cannot hide our thoughts from Jesus. We might be able to trick people into thinking that we are good Christians by going to church or wearing Christian t-shirts. But we cannot trick Jesus. He knows the hearts and the motives of everyone.

REFLECT

1. DESCRIBE A TIME WHEN YOU THOUGHT THAT YOU WERE DOING SOMETHING PRIVATELY, ONLY TO FIND OUT THAT IT WASN'T SO PRIVATE.

2. HOW DID IT MAKE YOU FEEL WHEN YOU REALIZED THAT YOU WERE EXPOSED?

3. WHAT THOUGHTS WOULD YOU BE ASHAMED FOR OTHER PEOPLE TO KNOW?

4. HOW DOES IT MAKE YOU FEEL THAT JESUS KNOWS YOUR THOUGHTS—EVEN THE BAD ONES?

VERSE 15

Has this ever happened to you? Someone says, "I can relate to what you're going through," but you know that they really can't. I would rather someone plainly tell me that they have no idea what I'm going through than to tell me that they can relate when they really can't. The death of a loved one is something that most people can relate to. However, until you've experienced the pain that comes with losing someone close to you, you really don't know how bad it hurts. Jesus knows how to relate to us because He lost someone very dear to Him.

Read John 11:17–37. Pay close attention to verses 33–37. During Jesus' life, He built many relationships, but He was especially close to the family of Mary, Martha and Lazarus. When Jesus learned that Lazarus was sick, He purposefully did not come to make him better. Of course, Jesus could have kept him from dying, but He didn't. He allowed Lazarus to die so that the people could see Jesus' power over death. Although Jesus knew that He would raise Lazarus from the dead, He also knew the seriousness of death. Jesus saw the pain that Mary and Martha felt, and He hurt with them. The Bible says, "Jesus wept." Jesus truly hurt because of His friend's death.

Jesus can relate to you when you experience pain of any sort. He comforts you when you hurt. Jesus wept with Mary and Martha. He genuinely cares for you and knows the pain that you feel. Even if you think that no one knows what you are going through when you are hurting, Jesus knows how you feel. You can trust Him and turn to Him in your pain. Jesus can comfort you because He has been there.

reflect

1. HOW DID YOU FEEL WHEN YOU READ VERSES 33–37?

2. HOW DOES IT MAKE YOU FEEL TO KNOW THAT JESUS OFFERS
COMFORT WHEN YOU ARE FEELING PAIN OR A DEEP SENSE OF LOSS?

3. ARE YOU HURTING? ARE YOU FEARFUL ABOUT SOMETHING? DO
YOU FEEL LOST OR DEPRESSED? HAS YOUR HEART BEEN BROKEN?
TURN TO JESUS RIGHT NOW AND ASK HIM TO EASE YOUR PAIN.
WRITE THE FOLLOWING STATEMENT IN THE SPACE BELOW:
"JESUS, I BELIEVE THAT YOU CAN TAKE MY PAIN AWAY. WHILE I
WAIT FOR THAT TO HAPPEN, I TRUST YOU TO COMFORT ME TOO."

Jesus answered, "It is written: 'Man does not live on bread alone.'"
Luke 4:4

There is a video circulating on the Internet that you might have seen. The clip, taken on a safari in Kruger, Africa, shows a herd of water buffalo at a watering hole. The buffalo do not see the nearby lions lurking in the grass. When the herd approaches the oasis, the lions attack. They do not attack the biggest buffalo; rather, they attack the weakest member of the group. The most vulnerable one. After a series of amazing events among the lions, buffalo, and crocodiles, the baby buffalo escapes. He did not, however, escape on his own. The herd joined forces and attacked the lions on behalf of the baby. Alone, the baby buffalo was helpless; but with the group, he was saved and made it out alive.

1 Peter 5:8–9 says that the devil prowls around like a roaring lion looking for someone to devour. Although he will attack, we can resist him and escape his schemes. Jesus taught us how to resist him because Satan tempted Jesus, too.

Read Luke 4:1–13. Satan used interesting tactics when tempting Jesus. He attacked Jesus where he thought He was most vulnerable. Jesus was hungry, and Satan tempted Him with food. Jesus had given up His place in Heaven for life on earth, so Satan tempted Him with power and kingdoms. If Jesus had simply asked the angels, they would have rescued Him, so Satan tempted Him with their obedience. The only counterattack that Jesus used was quoting Scripture to Satan. Simple, but effective.

Satan will often tempt you at your weakest point in life. He will find where you are most vulnerable and attack you. Although you may stumble, you can resist Satan the same way that Jesus did. Satan has no power over God's Word. Jesus was tempted, but He prevailed. He will help you prevail too.

REFLECT

1. IDENTIFY THE WEAKEST PARTS OF YOUR LIFE AND THE AREAS IN WHICH SATAN ATTACKS YOU.

2. WRITE DOWN THREE BIBLE VERSES THAT CAN HELP YOU IN THESE AREAS.

3. DESCRIBE A SITUATION IN WHICH YOU USED A MEMORY VERSE TO HELP YOU RESIST TEMPTATION.

"Why were you searching for me?" he asked. "Didn't you know I had to be in my Father's house?"
Luke 2:49

Would you say that you have changed a lot since you were young? The answer seems pretty straightforward. But in some cases, you're a lot today like the person you were growing up. Many people in high school like the same things they liked in junior high. And many people in college have the same likes and dislikes they had in high school.

The same goes for your spiritual life. If you develop good Bible study habits when you are young, they stay with you when you get older. This was also true for Jesus. His ministry didn't start when He was an adult. He laid the foundation when He was a young boy.

Read Luke 2:41–52. Jesus and His parents would go every year to Jerusalem for the Feast of the Passover. This particular time, however, Jesus chose to stay at the Temple and question the religious leaders. The leaders couldn't understand how He knew so much about the Scriptures. The reason that Jesus knew so much about Scripture was because He inspired the writings of the Scriptures. In fact, Jesus is the one about whom many of the Scriptures are written.

Although Jesus' public ministry began when He was about 30 years old, He didn't wait until then to start preparing. It's not like He crammed all night before He performed His first miracle. Jesus prepared His whole life for the plan that God had for Him. Similarly, you and I should start preparing now for the plan that God has for us. The way we live our life now and how seriously we take our relationship with Christ will determine how we live tomorrow.

reflect

1. WHAT ARE SOME GOOD HABITS YOU HAVE NOW THAT YOU WANT TO CONTINUE AS YOU GET OLDER?

2. WHAT ARE SOME NOT-SO-GOOD HABITS THAT YOU'D LIKE TO STOP BEFORE YOU GET OLDER?

3. WRITE TWO OR THREE SPIRITUAL GOALS THAT YOU WOULD LIKE TO ACCOMPLISH DURING THE NEXT WEEK, MONTH, AND YEAR.

verse 18

God made him who had no sin to be sin for us, so that
in him we might become the righteousness of God.
2 Corinthians 5:21

One of my hobbies is woodcarving. I carve little figurines and turn
them into Christmas ornaments for friends. I start with a plain block
of wood and then begin carving with a knife. When I start carving, I
know exactly what I want the figurine to look like. Sometimes I cut
big chunks and other times I make small intricate cuts. The process
from beginning to end is time-consuming, but the end result is very
fulfilling.

Now it's time for a vocabulary lesson. Have you ever heard the word
justification? This is a legal term that means to declare someone to be
not guilty. What about the word righteousness? This word deals with
God's way of making people right in His own eyes. Finally, what about
sanctification? This is the process of becoming more like who Jesus
wants you to be.

Now, with these definitions in mind, stop and read 2 Corinthians
5:21. Here is how it works. God has justified us (declared us as "not
guilty") through Jesus' death on the cross and resurrection from the
grave. We are made righteous (right in God's eyes) through sanctification (the process of becoming who Jesus wants us to be).

A woodcarver was asked the question, "How do you carve an eagle?"
To this he replied, "It's easy. You take this block of wood and cut away
anything that doesn't look like an eagle." Sanctification is very similar
to a block of wood in a master carver's hand. The carver chooses the
wood and then makes it into a masterpiece. He looks past the formless
block of wood and sees the wonderful end result. Sometimes the process is painful and takes a long time, but eventually the block becomes
a masterpiece. Since you have been made "not guilty," God wants to
make you into the person that you should be.

REFLECT

1. HOW DOES IT FEEL TO KNOW THAT GOD IS SHAPING YOU INTO A MASTERPIECE?

2. IN WHAT AREA OF YOUR LIFE IS GOD CARVING AWAY BIG CHUNKS TO MAKE YOU LOOK MORE LIKE HIM? WHAT ARE THE SMALL INTRICATE CUTS THAT HE'S MAKING?

3. TAKE THE THREE VOCABULARY WORDS FROM TODAY AND DEFINE THEM IN YOUR OWN WORDS. WRITE DOWN WHAT THEY PERSONALLY MEAN TO YOU. THEN READ THEM TO GOD AS A PRAYER OF THANKSGIVING.

VERSE 19

> But he was pierced for our transgressions, he was crushed for our iniquities; the punishment that brought us peace was upon him, and by his wounds we are healed.
>
> *Isaiah 53:5*

There was an article in a California newspaper several years ago about a 16-year-old girl that had just received her driver's license. She was driving by herself, enjoying the freedom of the open road, when she lost track of her speed. As she topped a hill, she saw red and blue lights flashing in her rearview mirror. The policeman pulled her over and gave her a speeding ticket. Wanting to appeal the ticket in court, she showed up and was denied by the judge; she was guilty as charged. He issued her a fine of several hundred dollars for the price of the ticket. What makes this story unique is that after issuing the fine, the judge stepped off the bench. He removed his robe, pulled out his wallet, and paid the fine. The judge was the girl's father, and he paid the price of the ticket for her.

Read Isaiah 53:1–5. Try something different today by reading it out loud. Sometimes it helps to hear or see things in a fresh way when we do something besides what we're accustomed to doing.

The price of sin costs much more than a speeding ticket. Paul tells us in Romans 6:23 that the price of sin is death, but the gift of God is eternal life in Christ Jesus. We are all guilty as charged in our sin. Jesus paid the price for us by dying on the cross. This passage in Isaiah prophesied Jesus' death. God gave these words to the prophet Isaiah so that the world would expect a savior. Jesus was that savior.

Each of us deserves the kind of punishment that Jesus endured. We are the guilty ones. Jesus took our place on the cross as payment for our sinful nature. Therefore, we should always remember Isaiah's words. We have peace and eternal life because of the punishment that Jesus received.

reflect

1. THINK ABOUT A TIME WHEN SOMEONE TOOK YOUR PLACE AND WAS PUNISHED INSTEAD OF YOU. HOW DID IT MAKE YOU FEEL?

2. HOW DID YOUR ATTITUDE TOWARD THAT PERSON CHANGE AFTER THEY DID THAT FOR YOU?

3. HOW DOES IT MAKE YOU FEEL THAT IT WAS JESUS WHO DIED ON THE CROSS INSTEAD OF YOU?

4. WHAT ARE SOME OF THE DAILY THINGS YOU DO THAT REFLECT THE WAY YOU FEEL TOWARD JESUS' SELFLESS ACT OF LOVE?

verse 20

While they were eating, Jesus took bread, gave thanks and broke it, and gave it to his disciples, saying, "Take it; this is my body."
Mark 14:22

I have always loved Thanksgiving, but after I got married I think that my love for this holiday bumped up a notch. See, for years I only had one Thanksgiving meal at Thanksgiving. But since I've been married, I have two every Thanksgiving. How awesome is that? Two turkeys, two sweet potato pies, and two tubs of dressing make me salivate every time. I do love the food. But even more than that, I love the thought of gathering around a table with family and friends to enjoy a meal together. Some of my fondest memories as a child are from Thanksgiving with my grandparents around a dinner table. Those times were special. As I read today's passage, I wonder if Jesus felt the same way?

Read Mark 14:22–26. Jesus was speaking metaphorically when He told His disciples that the bread was His body and the wine was His blood. Jesus knew that the coming night would be special because it was His last night before He was crucified. He wanted His disciples to remember that night, so He gave them something to remember Him by—the food they ate. Wine and bread were common at meals in Jesus' time. Yet He chose those ordinary items to represent His extraordinary sacrifice so that every time they ate bread and drank wine they would remember what Jesus had done for them.

When we say the blessing or give thanks before a meal, it should involve more than thanking God for the food we are about to eat. We should remember the sacrifice that Jesus made for us on the cross. Just as eating is something that we never forget to do, neither should we forget what Jesus did for us. So, next time you sit down to a meal and say the blessing, remember to thank Jesus for giving Himself for you just like He provided the food before you.

REFLECT

1. WHAT ARE SOME OF YOUR FAVORITE THANKSGIVING FOODS?

2. WHAT GOOD MEMORIES HAVE YOU SHARED WITH FRIENDS AND FAMILY AROUND THE DINNER TABLE?

3. WRITE DOWN FIVE REASONS WHY YOU ARE THANKFUL FOR JESUS.

VERSE 21

When he had received the drink, Jesus said, "It is finished." With that, he bowed his head and gave up his spirit.
John 19:30

Let's play a little game. I am going to give you a list, and you should respond by telling me what they have in common. Here we go:

· YOUR ELEMENTARY SCHOOL YEARS
· PRESIDENT GEORGE W. BUSH'S TERM
· THE YEAR 2003
· DINOSAURS
· THE ICE AGE

Do you have any idea? Here's the answer: These things are all finished. They have been completed, and nothing more can be added to them.

Read John 19:28–30. John 19 is all about Jesus on the cross, His earthly ministry has come to an end. Jesus' goal while on earth was to restore people to God. The only way to accomplish this was for Jesus to take on the sins of the world. The catch was that Jesus had to die when He took on this burden because the penalty of sin is death.

My favorite part of this verse is that Jesus "gave up" His spirit. No one took Jesus' life—He gave it up. He was obedient to the purpose that His Father had sent Him to accomplish. He was obedient even to death. This act of obedience completed the work that He had set out to finish. While on the cross, Jesus proclaimed that His work was finished. This phrase, "It is finished," is the most comforting word that Jesus could have said on the cross. This phrase gives us life and access to God.

Jesus had to die. Although He knew that it would be an agonizing process, He was obedient and looked past the process to see the end result. Sometimes the process is hard and not much fun while we are in the middle of it, but finishing something is always a good feeling. Jesus knew that if He quit before He finished that you and I would have no hope of salvation.

Following Jesus is going to be hard, but being obedient is worth it.

reflect

1. WHAT ACCOMPLISHMENT ARE YOU MOST PROUD OF?

2. WHY IS FOLLOWING JESUS DIFFICULT AT TIMES?

3. WHEN HAVE YOU BEEN OBEDIENT TO JESUS AND REWARDED AT THE END?

verse 22

> For we do not have a high priest who is unable to
> sympathize with our weaknesses, but we have one who
> has been tempted in every way, just as we are—yet was
> without sin. *Hebrews 4:15*

Counterfeit money has always intrigued me. Don't worry. I don't have any and have never even possessed any. (Not that I know of, at least.) Yet it is still an interesting concept to me. This is how I understand it: You want to buy something, so you take real money, make a copy of the real thing, and try to pay for whatever you originally wanted. I've never really understood how people get away with doing this, but I know that it happens all the time. It's funny to me that no matter how close to the real thing counterfeit money may appear, it's still a copy. It's worthless unless you want to start a fire or take on a paper mache project.

In order for our sin to be covered, someone had to fulfill the Law. Not just some of it—all of it. Read Hebrews 4:15. Until Jesus came, no one had ever kept the entire Law. People didn't even come close. Even though they tried to keep the Law, the very fact that they were born into sin kept them from being sinless. Jesus, however, was faced with the same temptations that you and I are faced with, yet He remained sinless.

When Jesus came, He was the only one worthy of paying the price that would fulfill the Law because He was the only one who upheld the Law. Jesus did not come to do away with the Law; He came to fulfill it so that the price could be paid for our sins. Attempting to pay the price of your sins with anything other than Jesus' sacrifice is a waste of time. Jesus is the only "real thing."

REFLECT

1. WHAT ARE SOME WAYS THAT PEOPLE TRY TO PAY FOR THEIR SINS?

2. HOW DOES IT MAKE YOU FEEL TO KNOW THAT JESUS WAS FACED WITH THE SAME TEMPTATIONS AS YOU?

3. HOW DOES YOUR VIEW OF JESUS CHANGE NOW THAT YOU KNOW JESUS WAS TEMPTED TOO?

VERSE 23

You see, at just
the right time,
when we were
still powerless,
Christ died for
the ungodly.
Romans 5:6

There's a famous story that goes like this: There was a man who did not believe that Jesus had died for his sins. He could not understand why God would send His son to die for people who did not deserve it. While he was at home one day, it began snowing. The storm became a blizzard. Staring out his window, he noticed two birds caught in the storm. He could see that they were trying to escape into his nearby barn, but they kept flying into the window. He knew that they would surely die if they stayed out in the snow, so he went outside to shoo the birds into the barn. But they flew away. He opened the window so that they could get out of the cold, but as he watched from inside they still flew into the glass. He thought, "Those stupid birds could die out there. If only I could become a bird, I could lead them to safety." Right then and there he understood exactly why God had sent Jesus to die for the world.

We are powerless on our own. Jesus had to lead us to safety. Read Romans 5:6–8. There are not two roads to Heaven: one for good people and one for those who trust in Jesus. Jesus didn't come as an alternative route of salvation for people who were not good enough to get to Heaven. He died for all of us because none of us are good enough. Ephesians 2:8–9 says that we are saved by grace and not by works. Christ died for the ungodly. Sorry to tell you, but that includes you and me.

So, when you don't feel good enough to be a Christian, cheer up! You never were good enough—that's why Jesus died for you. And now you live in the freedom that comes from God's grace.

reflect

1. WHEN DO YOU FEEL MOST LIKE A CHRISTIAN?

2. HOW CAN YOU CHANGE THE WAY THAT YOU FEEL DURING THE TIMES WHEN YOU DON'T FEEL GOOD ENOUGH TO BE A CHRISTIAN?

3. WRITE DOWN THREE TO FIVE WAYS TO REMIND YOURSELF THAT GOD LOVES YOU EVEN THOUGH YOU ARE NOT GOOD ENOUGH FOR SALVATION.

I am not ashamed of the gospel, because it is the power of God for the salvation of everyone who believes: first for the Jew, then for the Gentile.
Romans 1:16

I am from the South, where college football is king. Everywhere you go, seven days a week, people wear their team's colors to show their undying support. Every Saturday in the fall, literally millions of people travel hundreds of miles to their team's stadium. On Saturdays in the South, elementary school-teachers paint their faces like crazed warriors, and preachers yell, "Hit him!" and grandparents curse as part of their favorite cheer; yet nobody seems to think this behavior is odd. Here in the South, we unashamedly support our team. Sundays, however, are different. On Sundays, sometimes we don't even get out of bed for church—and if we do, it is often the first time that week that we've opened our Bible. It seems to me that many people are bigger football fans than they are followers of Jesus.

Does it sometimes feel as if people are ashamed of Jesus?

Read Romans 1:16. Paul was the furthest thing from ashamed. He recognized the importance and power of Christ's gospel and let everyone know his support for it. He knew that the gospel was for everyone, and he wanted everyone to accept it. Paul was the epitome of boldness for the gospel. Jesus was more than someone he visited on Sundays. Paul's life reflected his love for Jesus. Why? Because Jesus had saved him and turned his life completely around. He could never be the same after he met Jesus. Jesus was important to him.

I wish that I had Paul's boldness in regard to the gospel. In fact, it is sad to say, but I wish I had my own excitement about the gospel as I do my Auburn Tigers. Supporting a team is so exclusive; you're either for us or against us. Salvation, on the other hand, is for everyone. Jesus offers salvation to all who believe in Him.

REFLECT

1. HOW DO YOU SHOW LOVE FOR YOUR FAVORITE TEAM?

2. HOW DO YOU SHOW THE WORLD YOUR LOVE OF JESUS?

3. WHAT ARE SOME WAYS IN WHICH YOUR LIFE CAN SHOW THAT YOU ARE NOT ASHAMED OF CHRIST'S GOSPEL?

VERSE

You may ask me for anything in my name, and I will do it.
John 14:14

In the movie *P.S. I Love You*—spoiler alert—the husband of Hilary Swank's character dies. He knew that he was going to die for a while, so before he passed away he wrote her several letters. She was supposed to read these letters after his death to help her deal with his absence. Swank's character, depressed with the loss of her spouse, felt like he was still around because of the letters. She felt like he was there because he told her things to do and trips to take so that she could get on with her life. I know that it's a chick flick, but I thought it was a neat story. (Okay, maybe I cried a little. But don't tell anyone.)

Read John 14:9–14. Jesus is comforting His disciples because He is about to leave them. He tells them that although He is going to be with His Father, He will still be with them in spirit. Jesus reassured them that His power would not leave them. Even though Jesus left earth, He gave them access to Him in Heaven. Jesus allowed them to ask for anything in His name and promised that He would give it to them. This statement was intended to prove that He was going to be where He promised that He would be—with the Father.

Jesus gives us the same access to God's power. I truly believe in the power of Jesus' name and that He gives us what we ask so that it will bring glory to God. I do not believe, however, that if I ask for a 1969 Z28 Camaro in Jesus' name that I will get it. Jesus knows I do not need it, and it wouldn't really glorify God. Jesus was referring to the disciples' needs for ministry and the promise of power even in His absence. Jesus knows your needs, and He offers you His power in order to meet them.

reflect

1.WHEN HAVE YOU FELT JESUS' POWER IN YOUR LIFE?

2. WHY IS IT SOMETIMES HARD FOR YOU TO BELIEVE THAT YOU
HAVE ACCESS TO JESUS' POWER?

3. LIST THREE PRACTICAL WAYS THAT YOU CAN REMIND YOURSELF
THAT JESUS IS STILL WITH YOU EVEN THOUGH YOU CANNOT SEE HIM.

verse 26

Let us fix our eyes on Jesus, the author and perfecter
of our faith, who for the joy set before him endured
the cross, scorning its shame, and sat down at the
right hand of the throne of God. *Hebrews 12:2*

My wife and I grew up in towns with lakes. She water-skied, and I
fished. Naturally, we both love being on the water. In fact, our first
purchase as a married couple was a giant yellow kayak made for two.
Nevertheless, whether fishing or skiing, one thing to remember when
driving a boat is to watch where you are going. If you look to the left or
right, you are going to steer the boat to that side. The best way to drive
in a straight line is to keep your eyes fixed on something stationary,
like a tree or a house or maybe even a tree house. The same is true for
your Christian life. But instead of a tree house, we look to Jesus, who
will never change. He will always be there to keep us on the right path.

Stop and read Hebrews 12:1–3. Verse 2 describes Jesus as the author and perfecter of our faith. That means that if we are to follow
anything by faith that it should be Jesus. Why? Because He not only
created our faith, but Jesus also makes our faith perfect. Hebrews
11:1 says that when we have faith, we are certain of what we cannot
see. What can we not see? Well, salvation for one. But we have faith
that Jesus gives us salvation. He makes our faith perfect because when
we have Jesus, we have salvation. Without Him, we have no hope of
salvation. But with Jesus, our faith is made perfect because He gives us
salvation.

People put their faith in many different things: money, sports, fame,
good works, other people, etc. We cannot depend on those things,
because they will all pass away. We must fix our eyes on Jesus because
He is the only one in this world on whom we can completely depend.

REFLECT

1. WHAT THINGS OR PEOPLE HAVE LET YOU DOWN AFTER YOU PUT YOUR FAITH IN THEM?

2. WHAT ARE SOME WAYS THAT YOU CAN KEEP YOUR FOCUS ON JESUS INSTEAD OF OTHER THINGS?

3. WHAT ARE THREE THINGS THAT CAN HELP YOU KEEP YOUR FOCUS ON JESUS IN THE FUTURE? WHO ARE THREE PEOPLE WHO WILL HELP YOU?

VERSE

Whoever finds his life will lose it, and whoever loses his life for my sake will find it.

Matthew 10:39

Jim Elliot, a missionary to Ecuador during the 1940s and 50s, was killed while ministering to the Waodani people. After Elliot died, his wife, Elisabeth, returned to the Waodani people and had incredible success with the gospel. Before Jim died, he wrote a famous quote in his journal that said, "He is no fool who gives what he cannot keep to gain that which he cannot lose." The story of Jim and the four other missionaries who died was recorded in a movie titled *The End of the Spear*. Jim surrendered his life to Jesus and in return gained a life that was eternal.

Read Matthew 10:39. Jesus told His followers these words just before He sent them out into the mission field. Jesus wanted them to realize that following Him was more than just saying that they were His disciples. He wanted them to know the importance of completely surrendering their life to Him in ministry. He didn't want partially committed followers. Jesus wanted those who followed Him to be His lifelong disciples. His words reassured His followers that even if they gave up their life, they would actually find it in Jesus. If they searched for their own life outside of Jesus, however, they would lose it.

Life outside of Christ is death. Even though following Christ costs you your life, you really receive life. If I live without Jesus, I die. If I live with Jesus, I have to lose my life to be with Him. Sounds confusing at times, but it's really pretty simple.

Jesus wants us to be His lifelong disciples. He demands that we give up our life, our plans, and our dreams in exchange for His life for us. You and I may not die on the mission field like Jim Elliot, but we have to surrender our life to Christ to receive abundant life.

reflect

1. WHAT SACRIFICES HAVE YOU MADE IN ORDER TO FOLLOW JESUS?

2. WHAT DOES IT LOOK LIKE TO "LOSE YOUR LIFE FOR CHRIST"?

3. HOW CAN YOU LOSE YOUR LIFE FOR CHRIST AND STILL LIVE?

Therefore go and make disciples of all nations, baptizing them in the name of the Father and of the Son and of the Holy Spirit . . .
Matthew 28:19

Have you ever been on a mission trip? It's a pretty cool experience, huh? I've been on both national and international mission trips, and they are equally amazing when it comes to seeing how God works. But I sometimes think that we have the idea that missions can only take place when we are on trips. Missions are not limited to the remote places of the world. You can be a missionary flipping burgers at your after-school job.

Read Matthew 28:16–20. This passage is known as the Great Commission. But somewhere along the way, the focus shifted away from what Jesus originally intended for His disciples. The action statement of "Go and make disciples" can be somewhat misleading because in the original Greek the only verb in the phrase is what's translated as "make disciples." The word *go* is actually a participle and can be translated as "In your goings." If we read it according to how Jesus actually said it, we shift our focus from where we do missions to how we do missions.

Making disciples takes time and consistency. Jesus wants us to make disciples wherever we are and not just on trips. Whether at your school, on your team, in your band, at your job, in your home, neighborhood, college dorm room, or wherever you are—in your goings, make disciples.

How do you make a disciple? Look at Jesus' model. He devoted His life to His disciples. He spent time with them. He taught them the Scriptures. He ate with them, walked with them, spent the night at some of their houses, and prayed with them. He didn't just show up for a few days, read a verse or two from the Bible, sing a song and then leave.

Jesus made disciples by devoting His life to His followers. That is what we are called to do as well: devote our life to the one we follow.

REFLECT

1. HOW CAN YOU MAKE DISCIPLES WHEREVER YOU GO?

2. THINK OF SOMEONE WHO HAS DISCIPLED YOU. NOW WRITE ABOUT WHAT THAT WAS LIKE. WHAT DID YOU DO? HOW DID IT WORK? DID YOU MEET WEEKLY, MONTHLY, OR DAILY? WHERE DID YOU MEET TOGETHER?

3. HOW IS DISCIPLE-MAKING DIFFERENT FROM DECISION-MAKING?

VERSE 29

Jesus looked at him and loved him. "One thing you lack," he said. "Go, sell everything you have and give to the poor, and you will have treasure in heaven. Then come, follow me."
Mark 10:21

As I write this book, our economy is sinking. People have lost billions of dollars. In a poor economy, everyone looks for safe investments. But there are no sure things. Risks are always involved. In fact, most investment disclaimers tell you that it is possible for you to actually lose your money. But in our passage for today, Jesus talks about a different kind of investing: that of investing your life.

Read Mark 10:17–31. Many times, people would come up to Jesus along the roads when He traveled and ask Him questions. This story tells about a rich young man who wanted to know how to get eternal life. Jesus' answer shocked those listening. What?! Sell everything that he had? And give it to who?! Why would Jesus ask him to do that? Because Jesus knew that the man loved his earthly treasure more than his Heavenly treasure.

In verses 28–31, Jesus says that those who give up something to follow Him will receive a hundred times what they gave up. That is a great return on your investment. Most financial advisors tell you to "diversify your portfolio" (spread out your investments) in the hope of gaining 10 to 12 percent over the lifetime of the investment. Jesus tells us to give up everything in order to receive a hundred times that much in return. Investing your life in Jesus is a sure thing.

This is not a prosperity gospel promising that God will make you rich. This verse tells us that the blessing might be "in the age to come," meaning Heaven. Many times, our blessing comes from giving rather than getting. God wants us to be obedient to Him and give ourselves to others. Whether it is money, time, or possessions that we give God, we cannot out-give Him. He will always bless you with more than you give.

reflect

1. WHAT THINGS ARE YOU HOLDING ONTO LIKE THE RICH YOUNG MAN THAT YOU NEED TO GIVE TO GOD?

2. WHY DO WE WITHHOLD THINGS WHEN GOD PROMISES TO BLESS US FOR GIVING THEM AWAY?

3. NAME THREE TO FIVE WAYS THAT YOU CAN GIVE MORE OF YOURSELF TO GOD THROUGH YOUR POSSESSIONS.

verse 30

For I was hungry and you gave me something to eat, I
was thirsty and you gave me something to drink, I was
a stranger and you invited me in. *Matthew 25:35*

The movie *Valkyrie*, which starred Tom Cruise, is based on the true story of the conspiracy to assassinate Adolf Hitler. Dietrich Bonhoeffer, the German theologian, was executed because of his involvement in the Valkyrie conspiracy, but he was not mentioned in the movie. As a pastor, Bonhoeffer believed that in order for us to show God's love to others, we had to serve them. He said, "Possessions are not God's blessing and goodness, but the opportunities of service which God entrusts to us." To him, merely telling about God's love and neglecting someone's physical needs was not enough. Bonhoeffer believed in actively loving people with service as opposed to passively loving them with our words.

Read Matthew 25:31–46. Ouch! This verse makes me cringe when I think about the missed opportunities to serve Jesus that I have had in my life. This story teaches us that whenever we serve others, we are actually serving Jesus. He also said that when we fail to serve those in need, we are actually failing to serve Him. This should change the way that we view people. When we view opportunities to help people in need as opportunities to serve Jesus, our attitude should drastically change.

How can we serve God without serving people? It's not like we can go out to the city streets and give God a blanket or a warm bowl of soup. Or is it? In fact, based on our passage, the best way to serve God is to serve people. Read Matthew 22:37–40. This is why loving God and loving people are so closely related. The way that we love God is by loving people, and the way to show God's love is by serving others.

REFLECT

1. HOW CAN YOU PRACTICALLY SHOW GOD'S LOVE AT HOME? WHAT ABOUT AT SCHOOL?

2. WHAT KEEPS YOU FROM SERVING PEOPLE WHEN YOU KNOW THAT THEY ARE IN NEED?

3. WHAT CAN YOU DO TO CHANGE THE WAY THAT YOU VIEW PEOPLE IN NEED?

VERSE

31

"I am the vine; you are the branches. If a man remains in me and I in him, he will bear much fruit; apart from me you can do nothing."

John 15:5

I love vineyards. My grandfather grew muscadines and passed the art of growing and pruning vines down to my dad. It intrigues me as to how grape juice, wine, and jam can be made from a single fruit that grows on a vine. It baffles me to consider the way that you can train a vine and prune it in just the right way to produce the best fruit. I love the picture of God as the gardener who prunes something that grows wild like a vine and then produces something wonderful. God's final product is a fruitful vineyard. What a beautiful image of a life of intimacy with Christ!

Read John 15:1–8. Jesus used the image of a vineyard to illustrate that we are helpless without Him. In the same way that we cannot have salvation without Jesus, we also cannot live apart from Him once we are in Him. Our calling is "to abide" in Christ, which is another way of saying "to remain" in Him. Abiding in Christ means living in Christ. We are called to take up residence in Christ. I'm not talking about a take-off–your-shoes-and-stay-for-a-while kind of abiding; rather I'm talking about bring-in-the-U-haul-because-we-are-here-to-stay kind of abiding.

When you believe in Christ, then you are a branch connected to the Vine, Jesus. The purpose of abiding in Christ is so that He can produce fruit in you. It's eternal fruit that will last. You cannot produce the fruit yourself. Your job is to be the branch and let Jesus, the Vine, do the work. This is what it means to abide: to see yourself as the branch and to remain in the Vine as He produces the fruit.

reflect

1. CONSIDER THE ROLES OF THE GARDENER, VINE, AND BRANCH, THEN STATE IN WHICH ROLE YOU USUALLY SEE YOURSELF?

2. WHAT IS THE DIFFERENCE BETWEEN PRODUCING FRUIT AND ABIDING IN CHRIST?

3. WHAT DOES AN INTIMATE LIFE ABIDING IN JESUS LOOK LIKE TO YOU?

4. HOW DO YOU INTERACT WITH THE WORLD DIFFERENTLY WHEN YOU STEP INTO YOUR ROLE AS THE BRANCH?

CLOSING

Wow! You made it. I'm proud of you for reading this whole book. You've just done something that fewer and fewer people are doing these days: finishing something. A lot of people start out strong on projects, goals, and even books, but few people finish. Way to go!

If you ever feel unloved, think again. Jesus loves you. He loves you more than any guy or girl and even more than your family or best friend. Jesus' whole life and the reason that He stepped out of Heaven onto earth was because of His love for you.

I hope that after reading this book that you know more about who Jesus is and what He did for you. It's pretty amazing stuff, huh? But Jesus doesn't want you to simply know about Him. Jesus wants you to have a relationship with Him.

If you don't have a relationship with Jesus, please talk to someone whom you trust, such as a parent or youth minister, and they will help you get started.

Keep learning and growing closer to Jesus by praying, reading your Bible, and hanging out with other Christ-followers. Jesus knows you, and He wants you to know Him and His character.

Thanks again for reading this book. May God bless you and keep you.

Your friend,

Bryan Gill

BRYAN GILL

Bryan and his wife Sarah live on Lake Guntersville in Alabama with their yellow lab Roscoe and their yellow kayak Yacht-See. He and Sarah met at Auburn University, and they have been married since 2006. (Sarah's identical twin sister married Bryan's best friend from high school two weeks after Bryan and Sarah's wedding.) Bryan graduated from Auburn University with a bachelor's degree in communications. He also has a master of divinity degree from Beeson Divinity School at Samford University in Birmingham, Ala. When he is not writing or traveling to preach, Bryan spends his time practicing amateur photography. And when he's not shooting pictures, Bryan is probably hanging out with Roscoe, monopolizing Playstation 2, or blogging at **bryan-bigdreams.blogspot.com**.

EXECUTIVE EDITORS
Andy Blanks
Becca Davis

COPY EDITOR
Jason Odom

PUBLISHING ASSISTANTS
Lee Moore
Janie Walters

GRAPHIC DESIGNER
Laurel-Dawn Berryhill

ART DIRECTOR
Brandi Etheredge